Sapello Son

Editors' Selection from the 2022 Frost Place Chapbook Competition

Sapello Son

poems

Alejandro Lucero

BULL★CITY
PRESS
Durham, NC

Sapello Son

Library of Congress Cataloging-in-Publication Data

Names: Lucero, Alejandro, 1993- author.
Title: Sapello son : poems / Alejandro Lucero.
Description: Durham, NC : Bull City Press, [2024]
Identifiers: LCCN 2024002296 | ISBN 9781949344516 (paperback)
Subjects: LCSH: Rural families--New Mexico--Poetry. |
Sapello (N.M.)--Poetry. | LCGFT: Poetry.
Classification: LCC PS3612.U2547 S27 2024 | DDC 811.6--dc23/eng/20240117
LC record available at https://lccn.loc.gov/2024002296

Published in the United States of America
Book design by Spock and Associates

Author photo: Hannah Szwarc

Published by BULL CITY PRESS
1217 Odyssey Drive
Durham, NC 27713
www.BullCityPress.com

Contents

When I search "Sapello,"   1

Portrait of My Dad, the Self-Taught Weatherman, with Hammer-
    Blackened Nails and Grito   3

Pop Quiz with Ninth Inning Sweats   4

Pawn or Sell?   6

Birthday cake with stars   9

Con Tus Ojos   10

Farm for Sale: Sapello, NM   12

Sapello Son   13

Searching   17

when an officer tore open the pink evacuation letter of his lips   18

Things My Mother Forgets   20

Elegy with Snake Twisting My Blistered Tongue   21

My Tocayo: The Other Alejandro   23

Mom's Chair   25

Letter to Alejandro Lucero from Highway 94 in Sapello, New
    Mexico   29

jenga night with missing instructions   31

Poem for my teeth. I can't keep / you   33

Busted Pandemic Sonnet for My Dead Dad   35

Sapello Xmas   36

Pawn or Sell?   37

Reverse Pregnancy   40

Back Road Dream to the Home I Keep Forgetting   41

for Mom, Dad, and Hannah

When I search "Sapello,"

for Carlos Martinez, who discovered and named the Sapello asteroid

you and your asteroid pop
up above news of the latest wildfire.

I recognize the jelled bristles and shadow
of your widow's peak, ignore the report of ash seeping into the water

supply I no longer drink from. Carlos, the box cutter
kid. You grew up between grocery aisles, stocking Little Debbies

at your dad's store. Why did you name that shrinking stone,
stripped by atmosphere, after our hometown? Why not

your mother? Hell, why not the red beads of the pigweed's
wind-stripped vine? Those flowers our ancestors picked

off their socks—private gardens between the boot
and hem. I name my torn-up sneakers *Sapello*

shit kickers. Give friends with one last chance the last name
(Sapello) in my address book. Driving home blackout drunk

is *calling a Sapello taxi*. Where we're from they trick calabacitas
from the brittle dirt with river water, plant framed photos

next to homemade graves. You chose to burn your eyes
with calculus, soothe them against the cool glass of research

-grade telescopes. Professor Martinez,
teach me about the joys of being a child in Sapello

obsessed with night. Did you butterfly a sleeping bag
each weekend, waiting for shooting stars? Collect crickets

in Coke cans for their company, their music? Professor, tell me
you rattled them, your makeshift mariachi band,

when you nodded off below that tapestry of stars.
I picture you as a boy gazing black holes into the galaxy,

safe from the cries of starved coyotes. Someone's chained-up
mutts shouting back across the field. Tufts of Russian thistle

we call tumbleweeds stuck in the small teeth
of your barbed wire fence. I want to find that old article

with a photo of my childhood home beneath the title, an iris of fire
rising in the background. Would you have refused the evacuation

orders, exercised your right to sit back and choke on the smoke of ponderosa
pines? I never felt the warmth of a fireplace. My Sapello was blown

pilot lights. My family too afraid to light a match in the winter
drought. The wind turned our trailer into a frozen harmonica.

When you first saw it move, yellow tail stretched
like a sentence, the name was ready on your tongue. Your little Sapello

burning across our cracked leather sky.

Portrait of My Dad, the Self-Taught Weatherman, with Hammer-Blackened Nails and Grito

His spit-tipped finger calculates
inches of pain. He screams
at the sun when Sapello bone

-dries. He knows wind will whip
our walls and the sky may bruise
to whorls of pink and orange. He reads

us promises off a teleprompter.
The forecast always comes late
at night. Above Chente's hailing cry.

Pop Quiz with Ninth Inning Sweats

When did you last hug your mother?
   A. Before she spoke and I yelled. The word spun from my mouth like a screwball.
   B. When the stitches of the word bitch came loose in her glove.
   C. After the leather softened.
   D. We didn't hug.

Where?
   A. Beneath contrails too high for her cut straw to reach.
   B. Above the bottle cap that got pressed into my left shoe.
   C. At the edge of Geneva Park, where we once played catch.
   D. All of the above.

What were her eyes?
   A. Fossils.
   B. A person in the street.
   C. Two Percocets lost under the couch.
   D. Short comas.

And her tongue?
   A. Still veined, curled like a monstera leaf.
   B. Dry as her toothbrush.
   C. Twitching behind her laced lips.
   D. Missing in photographs.

How would she finish this sentence? Hello, __.
   A. boy biting the hair from his knuckles
   B. answer me
   C. I'm your mother
   D. I'm back

How long was her hair?

    A. Her ears shivered.

    B. There were knots; they could snap the teeth from a comb.

    C. It woke me up once.

    D. It wasn't there.

What was her job?

    A. A botched C-section and bloody hospital sheets.

    B. The leading role in 9-1-1 calls.

    C. Both A and B.

    D. Controlling the steep pitch of a heart monitor.

Do you miss her?

    A. thing she once told me was to always

    B. the same person I would like to

    C. first thing in the morning and to never force an ending.

    D. On most days.

Pawn or Sell?

Look at him now, duct-taped side mirror
drooping like a sad mutt's ear.
His poor car
panting in my parking lot. Him dragging along
his boy, who puts fingerprints in the dust
of every TV screen.
This man I know from high school.

Stitches unraveling from his sweat-stained cap.
He probably hasn't taken a razor to his face
since graduation, but his features
still shine like my display cases.
I hear he lives in some mobile home
sunk like a tombstone in the middle of a field.

The first time he came in
he was alone, holding his guitar like a trophy
he thought I'd spit shine for the window shoppers.
He didn't remember me.

"Pawn or sell?" I asked
and when he said he didn't know the difference
I explained the agreement. The loan.
How I could sell these items
at a new price when they became mine
after twenty-one days. When he came back
too late for his small DVD collection,
I again explained collateral.
Every time returned early for his guitar.

Months later he passed the holding date
for his wife's ring. The hazel-eyed pot smoker
who skipped every math class. Still can't be counted on.
Still has his perfect nose
we all admitted we'd pay to smash.

He always remembered the teachers' birthdays
and sang stale songs in class,
and if in home ec he nailed the notes with a sweetness
old Mrs. Tapia had never heard,
he'd get out of rolling cold pie dough.

He stumbled
down the stairs in tenth grade on the way to gym class.
I was there, waiting for it. Finally, the moment
he'd never live down. I watched the way he slid,
landed at the bottom
without a bang or bruise to everyone's applause.
His body folded into a bow.
And here he slides again into my shop.

Loose strings rattling in the acoustic's case:
today must be a week before his payday.
No way it's the one he had back in the day—
I've studied the scratches around the fretboard.
I bet it's the only guitar he has—
no way his ringless wife would let him hold onto more than one.

No way that'd happen to me
if I had a woman. If I had time for women,
I might have ended up with my own boy
leaving his DNA in pawnshop dust.

I always wanted to lie under the bleachers with this stoner
and his friends, sucking down six-packs and bowls of brick weed
at lunch, hippie grenades popping
at our lashes. Voted Most Likely to Be a Movie Star.
Least likely to sign his name in a yearbook.
Every month, he brings in that out-of-tune acoustic.
Before I can ask, he says *pawn*.

Birthday cake with stars

instead of candles. Mom never likes the melting
wax on her countertops. She has the blues
and lets them bleed into her vanilla-cracked canvas.

Hannah and I twist our tongues around
the eggbeaters when mom is done baking.
Her sugar milk circles our mouths.

Every year, after a homemade red velvet, we lie
on the lattice-panel porch and watch the stars
fall from the sky. Each one a tumbling,

unspoken wish: *For mom to be ok. For mom to*
bake forever. That Hannah sees you falling too. Miles away
from the rest of the world, in Sapello, the cheatgrass

growing wild around us, we watch the Little Dipper shovel
the shards of other stars behind itself,
like a boy cleaning a sidewalk alone,

until our sleeping bags turn cold around our toes
and the bag of chips between us goes stale. Right now,
I have more wishes in me than the copper-spiked

water in a well. My head filled with pennies,
her blurry face clear in the water.

Con Tus Ojos

That's all the Spanish my dad taught me
on car rides from basketball practice.
With your eyes, son. Use your fucking eyes.
Another sharp bounce pass slung
through my hands out-of-bodied.
I'm watching the play unfold. My dad
in the bleachers, the coach's whistle
vibrating off our skulls. *Con tus ojos,*
son. The car otherwise quiet. I felt
six again. A boy still without much
hair below the eyes. That day in my
sister's bedroom, we played with her
Barbies on the floor. The back of my thighs
itchy from the hairs woven into
her carpet. Aaron Carter shirtless
and puka-shelled in the ripped
poster above. With his voice
dad kicked down her door, told me
never to touch those thin
plastic legs or drive that hot pink
convertible off a mountain of
blankets again. He marched me
out to the kitchen, white-knuckle
steering my shoulders toward
the chair he pulled out from under
the table, like a root six years overgrown
in dirt he didn't recognize. He made me
watch him peel all the green chile
from our freezer. *Watch how I do it,*
son. He pinched the stem so tight

the nails of his thumb and forefinger
lost all their pink. With my eyes
I saw the softness in his blood
harden into white. Seeds too hot
to touch fell from the tips. Con mis ojos,
I saw him becoming the man
he wanted me to be.

Farm for Sale: Sapello, NM

Past the long-abandoned Church de San Rafael and through that cemetery where the old gate creaks when the young children dig near their ancestors' graves, along that trickling river where fat trout once splashed, shaded by the Jicarita mountains,

an escaped alpaca eats what's left of that blackberry bush the poor farmer's wife hasn't picked in years. He's already forgotten the taste of her pies.

Her red chile now comes in cans. All his livestock is sold. All his crops are harvested.

The nearby cottonwoods have retired. In her small bedroom, the farmer's lazy daughter draws eyebrows that arch like an open book. She talks about running away

as the grease from a burnt cheese taco drips on the floor at the cafe two miles up that main street with no name.

Once Daddy sells the place, she says into the glass of her makeup-smudged mirror. That bunk bed she sleeps in alone creaks too.

The farmer's son and his friends play ball on that basket bolted to the barn, their slender arms brown and ashen. Their teeth plastered with dust.

He doesn't want to leave his friends but wants to shoot hoops on pavement, not dirt. And besides, the adobe bricks of their home are crumbling fast and those gaps between the slats of the house's frame now show the stars in the desert dark sky.

The poor farmer could fix the roof and those walls, he could run out that thieving alpaca. He's just waiting for an offer.

Sapello Son

A family, no farm, a bottle

emptied; drunk till the thinnest brown moon
half-circled its base.

Outside, the Sapello sun robbed the land
of its fruit and flower. All the rainfall sucked
back through some straw
in the sky.

The clouds fat
with what they wouldn't give us. We once heard cackles
between the gaps
in the stratus. We saw a fire
start out of drought, felt
the smoke bruise our eyelids. Purpled
and puckered, those petals withered too. Inside,

a television buzzed
into the cold mornings.
Between the bathroom walls
a cut straw plugged
Mom's nose. Two more pills always tucked
inside her menthol pack.

A dry wind would kick
our roof at night. We woke up next to notebooks
scribbled with another night's dream.

Dad kicked doors. Slammed them

on his own fingers.
His voice broke us
down like that plastic Christmas tree
hiding in the closet.

Except for those weeks we saw the red lights glow
from the highway

just like you did.

***

Searching

again, for some galactic rock, Hannah unstuck
the glass from her eye—said *there is a heaven*. It sounded
like the last second of a kiss. If our parents could see us bent

-necked, scanning the sky from the other side of the moon,
that pocked curve hovering between us, they'd laugh
at the toy telescope. One Christmas they walked

it out under a jacket. Wrapped it in newspapers. Called it a family
present. I made them a picture frame with popsicle sticks. White
glue bubbled up where the red-glittered flats overlapped. I avoid

churches now. That first row pew, pew-pewing away.
Wood marbled smooth by asses in dress clothes. A black tie splitting
the hologram of my presence. A priest's voice vibrating off

the stained glass with every thud of *Our Lord*. Grief
clutching in our necks, held there by the off-tune echoes
behind us, chanting our parents off to the cosmos.

With the telescope, we could see into our neighbor's home
but never looked. We didn't want to watch them unsnake
the garland off their tree. We pointed it at our parents' new planet.

But the toy couldn't reach. It stopped at the moon. Every crater,
a pocket of loss our fingers couldn't pry. We set our telescope
on its wide lens; its tapered body standing like another hollow steeple to avoid.

when an officer tore open the pink evacuation letter of his lips

my front door an eyelid width cracked when he told me to get out

in a half hour flee the wind fed fire strawberry tipped trees grass gone

jasper brush stroked across the dead fields a burned

moon tongue slipped its blisters down my sweaty

clavicle i combed every coin from the kitchen that day left a half gallon

of milk to thicken in the unplugged refrigerator i never

heard home without its hum my laundry finished its wash cycle musty

shirts love the metal belly of a melting machine those clothes

aren't mine any longer wildfire smoked in oak-fueled

flames i didn't know could grow hotter when fed a family

home turned ghost town plot cigarette stamped x on gas station maps ash-

lined roads winding like intestines they can be heated white hot and stay

the same dirt paths knotted around pine rows separated like headstones

now coat tree bare the officer pointed past the smoke-

choked sky said to drive toward a town beneath the clearest clouds but if i could no longer   smell my fingerprints   singeing off the wall-

paper shedded hair melting   into the living room   carpet i should pull over

i might   have gone one memory   too far

Things My Mother Forgets

The boy who grew a mustache sitting under

his desk in seventh grade. My dirty palms

staining her door frames. How her nose controls the direction

of a cut straw over our bathroom counter. The pill dust

lapped up with her ring finger. She forgets hiding her rig

under the sink, behind that shampoo bottle

we never open. How every day I check if it's still there.

The stench of mold I catch ducking my head

beneath the pipes. Those movie nights we mock

the attractive. The two pieces of popcorn lost

under the couch. She might remember the green chile stew

she makes some evenings but not my stomach.

The pork but not my jaw breaking it apart. She forgets

my voice. The lisp I tuck behind

my tongue on the school bus. How she taught me to hold my tongue

back behind the stalls of my teeth if I say

horse. Or if I utter another *s*.

She forgets other animals too. The family

cat curled like a pubic hair on a bedsheet.

The dog that runs off more than she does; how they always come home

with fresh cuts on their chins. She forgot her address

once. A policeman called. Dad and I met him in a parking lot, my mother waiting

in his back seat, smoking a cigarette she forgot to light.

Elegy with Snake Twisting My Blistered Tongue

My mother was a forest of dead trees
longing for fire. All her recipes

you   lost

the   chain   she   gave   you   in   a   pool

for self-poison blackened in a stalled Rolodex.
She told me to hide the ash

of   dead   pine

needles, yanking   at   the   deathbed

under my nails, wait for a meteor shower
to wash it out. She asked me to wet her neck, pour my last

gift   as   you   walked   through her

one   last   time   (you   could   never   recover

raindrops to feed her twisted cottonmouth
river. She burned herself down once

I ran dry. Under the charred canopy of fringe on her forehead,

that   *glint*   *)*   *those*   *tarnished*   *gold*   *links*

matching   *your skin the*   *underside*

of an unlatched snake   *circling*   *through*

the shade of another burning body.

My Tocayo: The Other Alejandro

after Sandra Cisneros

You, the other Alejandro Lucero of San Miguel County,
born between 1900 and 1901. A tough tocayo to trace.

Just twenty-nine or thirty when the US census first published your
name, inked it in above your wife's, your occupation,

and your race, which they called white. Between bales of alfalfa, our name
could be called by a grandfather, could bring a foot of floss

from the bathroom to tie off a calf's umbilical cord. The mucus
and blood coating the fingers we wipe off on the same brand of jeans.

Below pine trees shaking in the Sangre de Cristo Mountains,
our name echoes from the throats of friends as we

round home plate on barn-made bases. But that 1930
Census says you were the head of the house. No time to play.

Married, and a father at twenty-nine or thirty. A farmer, like my grandpa.
Perhaps you were one of the first to give the cows

in New Mexico corn and bran for sweeter milk.
Maybe you just picked the snap peas and chased

the magpies off your grandmother's squash, like me.
What did the soil of our name taste like to you, tocayo?

How did your wife say it during sex? How did she maneuver
around our third syllable—harsh exhale of a laugh?

That *j* you replaced with an *x* in 1940 on the next census,
showing the names of your six children. Five in ten years.

Three girls. Three boys. Antonio, Banarito, Lorenza, Consuelo,
Cecilia, Evangelina. So many chances to pass on our name,

to give it another gust of wind, another footprint in the dust.
Why did you deprive Sapello of another Alejandro?

Were you afraid the name would bind them to your home like a nail-
head pounded flat into the wall? That it couldn't fend for itself in cities

far from the farm? You could have passed it on like a watch.
It's mine now. Until it's time to call my own tocayo to the barn.

Mom's Chair

On her chair, Mom would sag like a melting

candle—unlit. Bogarting

those Pall Malls that turned our curtains

to coffee

filters. Turned my sister and me into mourning

coughers. The moths

living rent free along the lace died from the smoke.

To us

that made them secondhand siblings. We buried them in toilet

paper coffins,

played a scratched CD, sang them down a drain.

We thought

it was rude to change the channel then turn

to stone

in front of your kids. Mom, the Lincoln Memorial

with a beauty

mark. Always so unsteady on her planet

that never spun.

She never drooled but blood once trickled

from her nose.

I dabbed it with a kiss while my sister wasn't looking. A cut straw still

in mom's pocket.

The front of her pants lightly dusted

like a chalk tray.

She got itchy. Not bugs under the skin, an itch

that melted

under the nails. My sister and I picked at her

neck like

a lotto ticket. She sat with her eyes closed, insisting she

wasn't asleep.

The un-ashed cigarettes showered burn holes into her

chair. Homemade

craters on the arms. A homemade planet

we threw away.

***

Letter to Alejandro Lucero from Highway 94 in Sapello, New Mexico

after Matthew Olzmann

Here, your grandma still shares her savory sopapillas with you. Often offering me a bite too. She still sees you, her young pinto bean, through the screen of her favorite window, playing tag with those wild rabbits you could never touch. She worries you won't see or hear the cars speeding by; I want to tell her you're not here; that I let you leave us. But would she believe me, my concrete and gravel all crocodile cracked from years of being rolled over? I wouldn't.

Alejandro, this road, my road, has been silent. Tranquil. Still as adobe pots in a windless home. Does that bother you? You grew up near my stretch of mile markers and rumble strips, but left. Moved faster than water over windshields. Faster than the clouds packing the rain we need. I remember bringing you home on a noisy school bus yellow like the egg-washed sky we shared. Now I hear only bug-bitten leaves dangling on an outstretched branch.

Your grandma still sits in the quilt-covered recliner next to her fireplace. I watch her. Someone should. I even watch the embers of pinewood she had to ax down alone flutter against the warm glass window, like flies in a jar. She jokes about soil so dry it wouldn't recognize a water drop, about how she farmed snow peas till their shells wouldn't snap, and about being trapped in the *Land of Enchantment*. She never hears, but I'm the only one who laughs. She probably thinks it's just the echo of another car passing through Sapello for the last time.

Along my road, barn cats are snatched from a thinning alfalfa field at the owl's midnight cry. They hoot and hold the writhing felines close to their tongues. But the cats want to fly away; they don't mind being taken. No rainfall. No snow. These cats don't even have a puddle to lick. They are sick of eating gophers and mice mixed with the leftover Spanish rice sitting alone in the back of your grandmother's refrigerator. Just between us, I have never cared for it either.

Alejandro, if you're still reading, I want to tell you that every night, with the consistency of a heartbeat, your abuelita unclenches her fists. Palms empty, brown fingers curled like cursive from years of rolling your tortillas flat, before you used me to drive away.

jenga night with missing instructions

below a falling ax is a moment of silence   a family split
                skull first makes every woodpile
                an excuse for separation   in the name
                        of warmth   I could never gather
                my family together in one room   I asked
                my parents all the worst questions
        before their deaths   where can I bury the hatchet
                in this poem   will you get to sleep
        in   stiff-jawed eyelids hard
-ball laced   I lick my fingers to throw   we will still
                take turns tucking words into each other's ears
                        to see who can say *I love you* the softest
        right   until the air in our voices goes ghost
        isn't it here where I pat dirt above your urns   our last
                game of reverse jenga   how will we ever know
the winner   those warm walls between us   I wish
        I knew why we yanked at blocks that were never there
                why you never went looking for the rule book
                I did not think to ask   I did not think to ask
                        you never went looking for the rule book
I knew why we yanked at blocks that were never there   why
        the winner was those warm walls between us   our last
                game of reverse jenga   how will we ever know
                here isn't where I pat dirt above your urns   I wish
                        right until the air in my voice goes ghost
                to see who could say *I love you* the softest
        take turns tucking words into each other's ears   hard
                        -ball laced I lick my fingers to throw
                        stiff-jawed eyelids
                in this poem   will you get to sleep

31

before your deaths   where can I bury the hatchet

my parents answered all the worst questions

my family together in one room   I asked

for warmth I could never gather

an excuse for separation in the name of

split skulls   every woodpile makes

a falling ax a moment of silence   a family below

Poem for my teeth. I can't keep / you

because you still grind yourselves into glass / powder just to wake me
each morning. You grew into foiled wet dreams who knew / my mother
was dying before she did / her monthly stripping
for doctors; your quiet voice / the steady pang of my dull incisor. The texture
of her pinto beans dissolved / through our forks
before we could bite. Coated your crowns / in loose fibers clinging to their peel
like wet sheets. We couldn't catch / a nutrient. So we started eating
dollar deals out of brown paper bags. She only ordered herself / the fries. Teeth,
I let you turn off / -white like lotion rubbed into brown skin or a pill
-ow all sweat stained from pent / -up mornings. Remember how
I licked the shovel-shaped backs / of you every time I saved Mom
and me a table, while she pissed away / her bloat. Liquor drenched
potatoes in the pockets / of her molars, you'd gnaw
holes into the meat of my cheek / when she'd leave
her ketchup splotches to buy another / plastic pint across Ruptura Street.
You held my tongue / tightly caged in your dental
arcade with no games. I couldn't / call her
back to our spot below / the arches. All my wisdoms
extracted, the first eighteen years with you were lessons / I ignored. Mournings
wasted, hoping for sex dreams to finish into that sad fabric / of cheap boxers.
To come alone, unconsciously, with only a blanket's / touch, Mom
wasting herself away on the other side / of that thin shared wall. I still reminisce
about my first / set. Your predecessors. The deciduous babies she
collected in that pill bottle with the label / picked clean.
Those small, unstained beginnings forced / through
my gums. Snapped out peacefully / in the mealy neck
of a pear. Tugged / by the worn-down bristles of my brush. Dropped
into the black-hole crevice / of a McDonald's booth. I spent all the quarters
she left / on my nightstand. I write you broke

-n, searching, once more, for her profile / in a pile of change.
When you grew back, she started using / the word *permanent*. Dear sweet

pearls of my maw, she knew nothing / was.

Busted Pandemic Sonnet for My Dead Dad

You taught me how to touch you like a house
of cards. Focus my breath away from the tilt

of your neck. They painted the coils of a ram's horns Tar Heel blue
for that last football game we saw. The fuzzy picture dying

to fade away. The way you hit ~~the hard side of our TV~~
made me flinch. But it worked, didn't it? Your "love

tap." You saved every receipt. Desk drawers stuffed with evidence
of all you spent on razor blades ~~never used~~. I barely saw your hair

under that Broncos cap until you asked me
to cut it all off. *Leave the beard*, you told me, rusted clippers humming

too close to your cheek. I bought another pack
of masks today, Tar Heel blue. (You've missed so much

bullshit). Men on ESPN said we shouldn't wear them; cosmetic as painting ~~that alpha~~
~~=keratin we can't shed.~~ Cheers to you, Dad, for not covering your hairy mouth

~~when I kissed you goodbye.~~

Sapello Xmas

Between the cracks of blinds, sunlight bothers us awake in our cold
trailer. The faucets are dripping. The pipes are begging

for steam to scream through. Nothing warm has trickled
out this week. The blue carpet matted like our greasy hair.

Near the front window, our plastic tree shivers when a sharp gust
slips through. A toothbrush hangs from Mom's chatty maw.

I'm glad she won't shut up today. My sister unwraps a few scratched
CDs, uncased. Their plastic bodies long cracked. The cover art

probably peeling apart in some puddle at that landfill in Estancia Valley.
Our trailer is a pound cake now all covered with snow. If you slice

it in half, longways, you might even feed a family for a night. Or you'll
open a broken box down its middle. Dad lights the oven and sits his dirty

socks near its open door. They look like toasted marshmallows being thawed.
I've only seen his feet that one time he taught me how to clean

my foreskin in the shower. When the water's hot, I open my skin like a gift.

Pawn or Sell?

We open the iron-bolted doors, pass a rack of jerseys and jackets

I know not to ask for.
                    I check on Mom's ring

                                        buried
                                        in its velvet
                                        graveyard.
Home Alone is always playing on the mounted 70-incher.
I imagine the Wet Bandits' hideout

would look exactly like this place: stolen bikes hanging like ceiling lights, greasy-
            looking gold coins,
faces warping in the funhouse reflection of watches.

Dad doesn't speak on the rides here
except to remind me to squeeze

                            his guitar case tight between my knees
                            when we head out over the ruts
on our dirt road.

He's stopped promising to fill them with gravel.

                                        Back in the shop,

                    Kevin screams and my Dad, second in line,
                            doesn't even turn around.

He doesn't see me

standing by some Nintendo games sitting in old shoeboxes
like rows of gray teeth

waiting for extraction. I think about pulling one out,
coming home to one of these consoles sitting in milk
crates. The buttons on the controllers
already rubbed smooth. This fantasy never changes
price.

I wish Dad paid me
my Christmas money back. Mom's cousin in Michigan unknowingly calls me

a good little saver,

My fake college fund grows
with every thank you note I send.
Maybe the pawnshop is where I keep learning
to lie. Other customers giving history to hairline cracks,

the mismatched china shaking in their hands.
Dad's up.

Just like every other time,
he doesn't even bother
negotiating.

He stays silent
until we are a handful of steps
away from the shop. His slim wallet
folded back into his pocket.

He opens the glovebox to a mess
of receipts and tells me
to move my leg
so he can stuff in another.

He says we need to stop
for gas and groceries.

I know the tattered bill he just traded for
won't make it home. That mom's pack of smokes
will have to wait. I never get to see the movie finish,

but when we leave I think about the bandits
and the pawn man watching them
fail each day.

Pawn or sell?, he used to ask. Now Dad just delicately unbuckles the case,
offering his guitar like a limp body.
                              The pawn man promises to hold it

for twenty-one days.   It only ever takes a Friday

                                             or two before our living

room fills with its ruckus again. Dad's wild strumming
of those brittle cords.

Reverse Pregnancy

after Matt Rasmussen

A doctor zippers Mom's belly together with a scalpel,
takes back the scar. Dad lets go of her hand and runs out

of the delivery room to erase his name
from the ER clipboard. He drops Mom

off at home before returning to his graveyard
shift. I curl into smaller versions of myself.

My fingers smooth. Mom's ankles deflate
so much all her friends stop asking about them. A new crib

gets dismantled with decreasing frustration. A carload of diapers
is restocked on the shelves at Tito's Quickstop. Mom inhales

the words *I'm keeping it*, rubs her last cigarette against a wall
until it cherries. The bottom of Dad's fist lifts the fracture

from a dinner plate. Lines fade on a test strip. They undress,
fall back into bed. The cells of their love pull apart.

Back Road Dream to the Home I Keep Forgetting

Sapello sky   open as a first breath   filled pink

tomorrow's weather   mismatched fence

posts   splintering into Ys   embalmed

with winter   the wind moves   summer skeletons

alfalfa turned tumble   -weed patches and pine branches

recite mariachi   music whistled   ancestors shuffling

playing cards   around a home   -made graveyard

in the field   behind the trailer abandoned   elk

bones and sheds   from old   hunts scatter under the fallen

needles Fragoso Ridge   pines dogs   chained a balding

trailer hitch   they wallow   waxing holes   into the thin vinyl

mobile home skirting   barn cats   morning screams

refrigerator scraps cold pintos   a wounded owl   top of a telephone pole

a crucifix   blood-dipped talons   dried   calls electrified dead

cells crossing   live wires   a fractured

family glued together   a single wide white car   parked in a black

-out   forgotten ride   home   I'm idling   still trying   to sleep

off a childhood   before walking back   inside

Acknowledgments

I'd like to thank the editors and readers at the following publications for first accepting these poems into their print and online platforms. Some pieces appear under different names and in different forms.

The Adroit Journal: "Birthday cake with stars" and "Con Tus Ojos"

The Allegheny Review: "My Tocayo: The Other Alejandro"

Booth: "Mom's Chair"

The Cincinnati Review: "Back Road Dream to the Home I Keep Forgetting" and "Poem for my teeth. I can't keep / you"

Crab Creek Review: "when an officer tore open the pink evacuation letter of his lips"

The Florida Review: "When I search 'Sapello,'" and "Elegy with Snake Twisting My Blistered Tongue"

Nashville Review: "Sapello Son"

The Offing: "Portrait of My Dad the Self-Taught Weatherman with Hammer Blackened Nails and Grito"

Quarterly West: "Busted Pandemic Sonnet for my Dead Dad"

Pidgeonholes: "Searching"

The Pinch: "Sapello Xmas 2003"

RHINO Poetry: "jenga night with missing instructions"

Salamander: "Pop Quiz with Ninth Inning Sweats"

Salt Hill: "Things My Mother Forgot"

Sink Hollow: "Letter to Alejandro Lucero from Highway 94 in Sapello, New Mexico"

The Southern Review: "Reverse Pregnancy"

Thin Air Magazine: "Farm for Sale: Sapello, NM"

"Poem for my teeth. I can't keep / you" was reprinted in *Verse Daily*: Editor J. P. Dancing Bear (online, 2023)

"Busted Pandemic Sonnet for my Dead Dad" was reprinted in *Best New Poets*, edited by Jeb Livingood, guest edited by Anna Journey (University of Virginia Press, 2023)

I'd like to thank Steven Espada Dawson, Nicky Beer, Wayne Miller, Joanna Luloff, Ahja Fox, Toby Tegrotenhuis, Jake Skeets, and all my friends at the University of Colorado-Denver and Arapahoe Community College; everyone at the 2022 Bucknell Seminar for Undergraduate Poets; and Dora Malech, James Arthur, and the rest of the faculty and my cohort at The Writing Seminars, for guidance, support, and belief in this project.

To Norma Jean Gryglewicz, Nea Lucero, Chris, Jo, Betsey, Frank, and the rest of my family and friends, too many of whom are no longer with us, who have cheered me on and watched me and this project grow. I am thankful for your love and support.

Finally, I want to thank my wife, Karen, as well as our late best friend, Nellie. I'm grateful for every challenge that's brought us closer and more excited for whatever is next, so long as we're together. This project exists because of your love. Your love, like the love from whom this collection is dedicated to, is why I am the way I am and why I found it in me to write this.

About the Author

Alejandro Lucero is a writer from Sapello, New Mexico. A 2022 June Fellow at the Bucknell Seminar for Undergraduate Poets, and former editor for *Copper Nickel*, his work can be found in publications such as *The Adroit Journal*, *Best New Poets*, *The Cincinnati Review*, *The Florida Review*, *The Offing*, and *The Southern Review*. He lives in Baltimore, where he is an MFA student in the Writing Seminars at Johns Hopkins University and an assistant editor for *The Hopkins Review*.